EDGE EFFECT

WESLEYAN POETRY

EDGE EFFECT

Trails and Portrayals

S A N D R A   M C P H E R S O N

Wesleyan University Press

Published by University Press of New England

Hanover and London

for my husband, Walter

❧

Wesleyan University Press
Published by University Press of New England
Hanover, NH 03755
© 1996 by Sandra McPherson
All rights reserved
Printed in the United States of America
5 4 3 2 1
CIP data appear at the end of the book

The images, "Center of Gravity" (cover) and "A Matter of Time" (part titles), are by Anne Griffin Johnson.

Today, an artist can be untrained, lacking in dexterity, emotionally disabled, even legally blind, yet still be recognized and rewarded for artistic excellence.

There may be no better way to understand this progression than to search for art in thrift shops, flea markets, and yard sales. There, amid the dental irrigators, stuffed animals, and coffee mugs, you're on your own—as are the unknown artists whose works are haphazardly offered. But if you search long enough, and are fortunate, you'll not only find something worth keeping, you'll also develop an eye that will enable you to recognize excellence in other unlikely places—in backyards, down dirt roads, in senior citizen centers, in homeless shelters—in short, wherever someone, however "unqualified," decides to be graphically expressive.

—Gene Epstein, "What Kind of Art is This?"

❧

The zone where two communities overlap, called an ecotone, shares characteristics of both communities and therefore is diverse. That is, the edge of a community is more diversified than its center, a phenomenon also known as "edge effect."

The region where the land and sea overlap is known as the intertidal or littoral zone. This region, influenced by the daily ebb and flow of tides, is one of the best examples of edge effect in the world.

—Allan A. Schoenherr, *A Natural History of California*

❧

Unidentified Woman #5: I say give him a break. He is trying. He's trying to express his art. But I will tell you, bring it on the inside. Don't leave it on the outside.

. . . .

Winfrey: Would you then move it on the inside? Would you—what would you do?

Mr. Guyton: No, I think it should stay on the outside.

—Oprah Winfrey Show, "Neighbor Vs. Neighbor,"
with Detroit environmental artist Tyree Guyton

CONTENTS

2

Trails

EDGE EFFECT

Choosing an Author for Assurance in the Night

    I hoped it would be someone
who, burning through her last mask,
debuting with the creases earned
    from its petrified pillow,
        would show me how
        to live persistently.
Reject (I asked) the hollow protection
    of your headdress,
        mystagogue, inspiritor,
            its copper
    wires and antelope skin,
its bronze or cam wood or coconut hair.

    But I have to turn
to the lean idol of this Day of the Dead
compulsive writer in her afterlife,
    whose own fine fittings have slipped.
        She's hung them up with her fencing mesh
        and catcher's grille.
She types:
        "I know now
        to be plain, with an occasional seed
            leafing out from my sutures.
    I am bony as a bridge,
a bare letter-by-letter pusher,

    assembled in angles
to span.
Death makes me direct,
    with a little ornamental nonsense
        of elbows and knees,
        if you call this death:
my twaddle still counsels
        though I have no ears to hook a mask on.

'Carver, coppersmith, make me a disguise,'
    you won't hear me saying.
    My typing fingers fly
up to my face

    like a plunging pianist's.
Accurate, flexible, but not bravura.
So for the sacred ritual
    around the fire
        I will not be chosen;
        to chant
one needs the scored shell of an artist,
        the scarifications
        of a decorator to look out through,
            pod eyes, tube eyes,
    to breathe through, to
tug an audience through with

    innuendo, wooden winks.
Now, I like my skull
but it won't get me the priestesshood.
    I like my skull;
        it got me here."
                    And here—
    close beside me.
The blood is running around in my hand
        to keep up with her messages
        from,
            it feels like,
    one of those colossal stones
that throw starlight.

1

Portrayals

Affirmation Against Critics

Defending the unreasonable, deranged
   design, as art of a different wellness,
as something wholly well only when it is wild,

led me to see it as an aesthetic
   testing those who never pieced a thing:
      Failing this severity, they went on

   making nothing and
judgments.
         Her children studied
the nonsense of the quilt,

perceived a disposition they would not
   morally change—it was Mother's
      calculations: She could not make

   a worthless order.
   She could not offer worthless color.
The worth of shape was icily debated.

   She only offered
her shape. Her discomposure.
      The oddity

was no flowering of grief we could
      name timeless;
   rounds and crosses she stitched

   authored the a-universal
      from actual shreds of her life,
launched tremendous wheeling power—

junk but not facsimile.
    (Joyous fabrics—each skirt
lifting lightly, a botany of gathers,

       bees going up sleeves,
    the heat shimmying through weightless red lawn,
yellow and magenta, coral and night-green—

       that is how the margins are colored,
should you sail there . . .)

Painting Self-Portraits with the Wisdom Project Women

What is my personal power symbol?
I didn't know then and I don't know now.
But I needed to brush it three times
on very large and visible paper,
along with an animal and a gift
of comfort I'd give to a friend (a teacup—
I can paint it easily).

                    Joyce
has her hearts and others have their dripping rainbows.
Dalene even has a knife. Of course
now it is three knives (no, two,
the composition is best that way).
The women no longer need to use a mirror
like the one my left hand tries to find
my face with while I pencil with my right.

Their faces are already daffodil
or modeled in contours of blue: Rage
and queenliness and that pretty darn sly
look of Donna's are some of their best.
They just don't water themselves down.
Whereas, pale pale purple
without even an object to flesh out, involve,

has become my personal power symbol.
A wash as symbol.
But the wash is like walking through a field
and waiting for the birds to land.
It is like the sky the mother pheasant
watches for cars as she waits to
cross her chicks to the next safflower field. The wash

is like water the rice plants
are up to their necks in.
And I have once again portrayed the outside world
for a self. It's a pretty picture, representative.
But "What is your personal power symbol,"
Susan asks, "You have one. You have to have one."

> *This quadrangle of knowledge*
> *that color exists?*
> *The tender way I do the hair*
> *of the brush?*

Then Shella paints a crown.

Eclipse Facsimile

It is cheaper than sitting for a portrait:
The Xerox shakes out a picture—

but of what presence?
An iron stove with heat waves tressing it.

This is a face, perhaps.
Or perhaps it has seen *behind* her face.

Had it worked, she'd be urging others to try it, too,
lay a cheek on the windowplate, make a jacket a blind.

Five cents
gets a roller of light and a shudder.

But anyone will show up sooty,
like a mud puddle kicked, or an ancient rubbing.

When she and her partner step out for the sun,
people huddle on every curb.

Each crowd has two sheets of paper
to tip and space.

Over the south sky a tin-colored shadow cuts
and cools mobs gathering around projectionists:

Crescents, all from one branding iron,
burn the center of each camp.

She takes her gray portrait from her friend's hand,
stings it with a pin,

and lenses the eclipse down onto his flat, shaded stomach. . . .

As it darkens, everyone is happy,

faces glow. The sun has drawn
the one forbidden place to look

on places closest to us.
As many times as the page will hold holes,

she makes a beam come through to him.
But is that image the sun? Is each one?

Can anyone keep loving it so? When is it rare?
Copies are everywhere.

The Study of Genius

Laurel and Hardy Convention, Las Vegas, 1992

I am passing behind one of five Ringling
Brothers clowns, the one with green hair
and white piping on billowing outline,
as he stands at the back of the convention
and watches the film.

He is sensing
the staircasing in his body,
the coiling within the standstill,
while two shadow-and-light gentlemen
goof with all the hopeful grandeur

of one's double-fat face and tasty pique—
his partner's pencil elementariness
and high-pitched sniffling
bringing the spat to a damp, shy close.
Green Hair follows every movement

for the years it takes
to bone this costume out as a human if.
The act feels so new, of these old two,
that he lives to know what makes it so.
While, to his right, the transvestite,

modeling his attention,
wears his study of the wives,
his Forties Schiaparelli suit,
fox stole, wartime entire costume change
of earrings, brooch, and hat,

his lingerie blouse complementing
the gray slender silhouette
of rationed jersey (square shoulders

mostly his own). And plastic shoes.
And those of us who dress up as ourselves

seem the slackest students, ready-to-wear,
unscripted as chit-chat, our gestures flat,
our timing countable by neither chimes nor jewels.
We can only revere
the elderly child actors on the dais,

tracking the other definition of genius,
that guardian spirit of earlier place and time,
watching reels of their creator-child,
re-running around, that scrappy, indefatigable guide
to the unrecoverable self.

The Clown

for Arthur Hamilton Smith

There, between Leakey's yellow fingernails,
was the first skull becoming human.
And the angels, who could use gold
paint, were also pedigreed in their time.
Whatever the order of beings, the clown
was roped off from our gods and our families.

Barren, a visitor of removable brains,
there under his blindingly pale face
(geisha layers—and yet nothing
is womanly about this Bubba)
shines a self to match, a blue and burning
spotlight determined to reach our gods

and our families. Sixty children are holding
their breath. He is as excited as fleas.
He falls with a bounce, a fish in his pocket
clangs, and he's somehow still dapper, the skinning
absorbed by gloves, and the laughter
directed at every kenspeckle part of him

stored in the fake shirrs of fat. To undo
the many-gored suit and the ruche, he surrenders
at home, feeling treated a bit short
of his won city. He keeps on
the face. Only turns off the light.
The mirror doubles the gleams.

The first time, he washed his face too soon,
his eyes wouldn't clear, he saw streaks.
His friends saw them too, real as ghosts,
white Tom Sawyer swipes, a superficial job of it.

So for now he sits down, t-shirt and gardenia
face, a corsage on a chair.

Outside, the old two-storeys look
from night-lamped features. No matter
how many heads sleep inside, restless
parties flirt in and out of its mouth,
a house's eyes are lit in a stardom
bigger and more solitary than any human face.

His eyes shuttle then, eyes within eyes.
He wiggles his mouth, a working model of his greater
smile. Somewhere are nostrils, very small,
how little air this man beneath inflates on!
And so curious does he become at last
he will bow into the soap.

Ode to Early Work

Of those who finally win notice,
of these artists it is said their early work
is either purer, more astounding,
or fainter, less filled in, too
central. Or all vision, little hand.

But I like them as I like late Auden:
home's in the meter, the pen's in a landscape
or a side-yard, the colored pencil shades
a written line. He could have drawn some words
in crayon (not all). Even enjambed stanzas

could be framed—in wood. Early Minnie Evans
is plump cat-faces whose ears
are humans; or sparse seedheads
of grasses from baptismal basins in a drought.
That line which comes soonest

shows the hand how blood-and-bone pristine
it is, but also proves to the dreamer
this is not a sleep plot, the hued dirt
of a line is awake for love.
Murry's first works were on adding machine tape;

Mary T. Smith's on corrugated roofing panels to fence the yard.
Now she paints on plywood works to sell.
One's dawning empty backgrounds count.
Too delicate colors, nascently gutting the white,
still scratch against each other.

Nor should all early work
be viewed in the morning. It is
in the grinding maturity of lateness,

the stretches of lightlessness, that early work
can bring the tact, tensility,

one lost in propounding, even pleading for, one's life.
Early work that commenced in
souls older than most lives,
first marks swirling toward too many lions,
or oafish compulsive scowling mugs,

or sweet roseate cheeks blotting up
a market of paper bags. Never mind,
keep going, keep moving, as long as you include
point zero in your work, as long as there
is no eraser at your genesis.

My Personal Hercules

I have no way to earn a living
but to find a giant horse
and make it stand in a yellow tent,
one harvest-amber town after the next,
beside the bigger and sadder bull
and the tiny, resourceless stallion,
Garboesque, lying on pale straw
in a sunken, untouchable court.

If my enticement is any more monstrous today
than yesterday, if it builds any more power
into its sides, if its red-gold plush
weaves any broader Belgian tapestry, if it
scratches its burgeoning knee with ever more giant teeth,
my living and my sadness will prosper,
dependent on death to chalk their height—
more chaff in a greater fringe of eyelashes.

Two-tone phallus, pink end proffered,
truck-tire-black tubing retrieving it.
Constant alfalfa, barrel of water quaffed
with tsunami tongue: It is happier
eyeing people to ignore
than is "Ten Thousand Hamburgers on the Hoof" next door,
happier than the paragon rabbit
nibbling its ribbon, blue.

We have no home, no hutch, no roost.
I am a brute. The horse
is mortal and majestic, magnanimous,
whose grandeur moves by trailer.
Named Hercules, nineteen hands tall,

two thousand seven hundred fifty pounds,
five years old and grown by tumor—
pituitary, once a cinnamon foal
in Florida, disproportionate poetry.

Spirit Writings

Murry wants to write; he loves the glyph flood of written speech; he cannot read; he invents a graceful script anyway, with water-color; his paintings are this way verbal and liquid; they present shapes of ghosts, washes for bodies; he reinvents the ghostwriter; his spirits' eyes are important—those who can't see he puts glasses on; he has inspected cursive and found it divine—full of intima-tion, moment, forbidding paraphrase. He feels God gives him

the gift to write, which mortals denied him; he has a great deal to say with his writing, pages to soak; where did he receive the an-nunciation ordaining him to lace streaming spiritual bodies with marchings that look like sentences; he says it is not his idea; he has the confidence of an ancient still-in-progress calligrapher who writes poems down the side of paintings; of Wang Wei, who mono-chromed, doubly, landscapes and poems; a feeling like that of the scroll of the moment hung in the alcove of a Zen tearoom.

This sheet looks like columns in a daily, with backrush rill forms, spreading delta channels; seems to represent many reportings, lots to speak out about; what needs to be styled into tablets, paper as well as stone; it is a violet-letter New Testament; Ghost with Glasses, Ghost with Orange Aura; faint thistle fingerprint—Murry's; no feet—a cross indicates a haint's body is

finishing. Murry can't read his Bible. Murry reads spirits. A cat will, abruptly, directly, step up to the spirit painting, stretch her belly along the drawn-out dissipation of the amethyst spirit's shape and paw (stained-glass-window-shaped paw) over and over the silken face of the demon (you can see where the dust is gone on the glass door to this closet of paper robes). The wraiths—there are four—respond with a strong stare. One has just left the fire to rippling backlight, without yet burning out.

God is going to put the written paintings together in a book. No changes to the text will be made. No proof marks will scratch the copy. The book will be bound, the writing be in color. The faces readable through fluid paragraphs will be orange, yellow, grape. The book will put readers in one binding with that which is read. The pages will be heavy like tatting, starched, the white showing through. The covers will be moss on laminations of bark. The book will come with a bottle

of water from Murry's well. The water will translate the chapters as it magnifies, as it slides along amplifying, preaching. It is not a novel; it is unfeigned utterance, import. There is neither first conflict nor denouement. Murder—the power of the lost—won't whole this birth. The mystery's detective dissolves on the horsehair and color crystals of deduction. The message seeks no ending, middle to middle. The handwriting of the on-and-on.

Reposoir

Four Legends for Mose Tolliver's "Flowering Tree"

I

My left hand is weeding millet out from under blue-blossoming
    rosemary.
As its spark enters my skin,
the bee squats in disgust, distraught.
Light passes out of its fur.
What if our last two acts are anger and sleep?—
just look at this hero.

But our earliest spurs
are pistils and fruit almost seasoned and childhood under leaves,
every color-mix proffered and breathed.

So I am reminded
here beside the tree
of the man with crushed feet.

2

Whether arching to the ground to set a bird down
or chalicing straight up into the sky, the tree
invites in, pours out, gallons of bees.
Roots rumple, pucker, rubble the soil.
The upper branches swim overhand.
No two blossoms flex alike
or look the same:
plain, spotted, streaked,
smeared thin, thin-walled,
ox-corpuscled, splotched, poppy, godoetia,
mint, effervescent, dressy, sun-embossed—

altogether atypical, omnifarious, heteromorphic.
Same tree. No synonymous rainbows.

3

At the beginning,
it was not the Lion of the Knowledge of Good and Evil:
it was the Tree. It was not the Emerald
of the Knowledge of Good and Evil. It was the Tree.
It was not the Sun of the Knowledge of Good and Evil. It was
the Tree. It hasn't yet become the
Bubble of the Knowledge of Good and Evil; it is still
the gallery of the Tree. It isn't the Book,
but it could be the Driftwood. It isn't
the Government of the Knowledge of Good and Evil.
It is the peppertree,
the valley oak, the banyan, the boojum,
the plumeria, the poinciana,
the date palm's ten-thousand flowers in a cluster,
the Norway maple's springtime shatter, its yellow lights as rain-
    shadow,
it is the Santa Cruz Mountains madrone axed by a man with no
    knowledge
of good or evil—
that red brancher which the landowners, out of onus
(but not knowledge)
toward Good (because he had five children) allowed
to be replaced with a liquidambar, mere furniture,
that didn't know the mountain,
instead of suing him—

thereby losing knowledge, true goodness, sacrificing
the peeling revelation of the madrone,
its white depending olla blossoms,
even the miller worms that swing
on gossamer (rain become flesh).

Under that tree, out of arbutus and redwood duff, I dug up a skull,
one cup's worth of knowing.

4

When you consider, lumberman,
preferring money to a tree,
consider the god prefers
the tree as home.
And people prefer the god as home
over themselves.

Developer, consider the petals,
all those love notes
slipped into the imprints of an artist's crutches
by April's armloads.

Outsider: Minnie Evans

Now, because of you, symmetry and asymmetry interest me *equally*.
Paints tinting the cisterns in which they mix
slosh and overflow, but you tend the garden gate.
You are so celestially symmetrical that if
you have a sun rising from the sea on the left
in your picture, you'll put the echo of a sun
rising out of the same ocean on the right, an island for their hub.

You draw portraits of spirits, mount them
on suit-box board and carry the crowd as a deck.

Those little wraith faces in leaves and fruit, cherrylike.
Or heads in urns, one face channeling fire into the mind above.

You were a domestic servant when you made these.
"Draw or die," said a dream.

A symmetrical thing measures itself
according to itself. Shoulders make a vase.
Wings have their own faces. Life-forms
share surfaces and rally into medallions.
Because of the admonition—
which didn't say, "Draw and live."

25 Jan 92: I've been in depression for days but felt a sudden rush of change—like the push of caffeine—upward—and the whoosh is associated with the draft of fire up one woman's head through her hair to the neck of the woman's face above—pentecostal chimney! The flame my cremation creates! The wings lifting me, the urn by its handles soaring. I am the head of the flame. I am handing it up, up, the expression of each wing, the stomping and clapping, the women in tongues, the women holding the women falling backward and upward, glossy glassy glossolalia, their eyes up where the flame goes, the hats dropping to the floor, decorating the hearth on which we dance.

Handles have to be wings —to lift their burden on their own —handles have to be wings.

And the path out of the vision
is asymmetry.

There it goes, all by itself,
daring its route away.

And out there facing the single fire,
the single sun,
is the one person
who is but one.

Outsider: Juanita Rogers

Except for when she's spirited away,
    she'll never leave
Alabama. Cohorts and tutelaries

    believed from the television
        line the one-room surrounding her womb
a cottage abortion smoothed

    into a huge
        tumorous study of pregnancy.
"Here": is pigment and mud. "Not here":

    Egypt,
        blue and clamshelled in her paints,
her azurite

    exotic continent, nowhere
        that does not spice and whiff
of the close range of pretending,

    a lapping
        coastline, rust and turquoise,
diminishing in the outermost. Which,

    however, she pretends
        at once to live in too:
"Way off somewhere . . . no houses on land

    only shells and rocks.
        In the shells
are pearls." An early world. But no dawn. Dusk

    with white loafers.
        A lonely place. Shell mounds. Fish midden.
Each shell as big as a loafer.

Bubbles or steam or sanddollars.
    Chalky salt crust.
Man powered with a pencil.

    She conducts steam's response to sun.
        Shore's to burnoose.
Because if you keep your Unbelievable into adulthood

    maybe you will do something
        against sadness
at its behest. In her ear a Mr. Stonefish

    says to paint. She does and
        doesn't end herself,
the world at Egypt; she pretends,

    authenticating
        a sun of persimmon bridge-rust,
night all around the sun.

Great Art, Great Criticism

Mattie Pickett, Quilter

Van Gogh as bedding —
a woman healer's starry night:
Pyres of crushed skirts,
of black and brown light, of blue
and hot pepper search-beams,
comfort my Louvre.
It is a strange thing to want —
for there is no scrap pomp;
and pins are left in the monument
of wide neckties.
There is no doctoral
unapplied comment of cloth
but shock of its fuchsia-loud
gag. Quilt talking, poem talking,
student speaking. The
persimmon-colored tongue.

Justin McCarthy, Naive

Pennsylvania 1892 – 1977

Tormented
by grace,
he had to
scratch at it,

leave
the marks
of his enthusiasm,
his best

imperfect
penstroke.
All to gain
a keepsake

of a yellow
bathingsuit;
of an iceskate
as the season

of pleasure
changes.
And especially one
figure, her skin

that doesn't
belong
in nature,
her diaphanous

pelt, her chiffon
hide, as if she were

pasted
into the golden

shade
of the pinewoods,
where the deer,
watching, redden

the creek
with their reflections.
Though he inks-in
her muffless

pudenda,
he forgets
any mention
of nipples.

Yet he gives her
the detailed face
of longing,
a face thinking

it veils
the longing
it reveals.
There is a reason

the awkward artist
can accomplish
such a difficult thing—
a reason the effect

is not accident
alone:
Facility
defaces longing.

Longing is
the one expression
skill masks,
polish ravages.

Lessons Learned from a Small Drawing
by Victor Joseph Gatto, Self-Taught Artist

If you cannot make a living from your art,
double the art, double any part

(but not the whole)
of the body of a woman,

multiply eyes in every head.
She'll never view you in a simple way.

If you cannot make a living from your art,
the freak is yours.

Think of your lady's two heads on your shoulder.
Make only what you cannot bear to part with.

Because you will not make a living from your art.

    My poems are my age, X'd out on their hanging calendar,
    where the pretty picture

    is not mine—mine's the gargoylish deadline
    (I hold my pen wrong too).

    And while the populace reads make-believe
    I swear to all true language

    each pate's an equal citizen, willing to work.
    One will perform the chore in fact you hired her for

    if you just let her other wit
    (the one that's made of poetry)

    come along.

Preliminary Designs

When you actually build it,
    it calls for repair,
      spackle, cedar, tiny hardware.
But not to know
how to build! Only to

    design! A fantasia. In
      the lookout tower:
        rotating, sky-lit, circular
compartments, glassy
clean surfaces, a museum's unmessy

    curio drawers, counters, rooms of
      every shape in Geometry
        II or crystallography—
garneto, the swallowtail
twin crystal (a good practical

    interior for reversible despair).
      Someone is just doodling
        arches, viaducts, mottling
low walls with yews,
water with shadows of causeways,

    deigning to design
      more heavenly
        cities than Heaven;
someone wants Rome *and* space
colonies, acute angles, rulered lines racing

    to a turret painted
      diffusive blue.
        It's the need to plan (not plant)
silhouette trees, gracile even weedy
aerials in roofs, posit glaciers in view,

to turn inside into out,
>front to back, make windows
>into walls. Or windowseats into
garden benches.
I built shoebox houses,

>crayoned woods chosen for their light,
>>snipped paper trellises, screens across
>>a porch or yard—open
enough for bees, finches, sphinx moths to pass through.
Pasted on black and white photographs

>of wet flowers against waxy leaves . . .
>>Preliminary designs:
>>They are where we dwell now
more than we will
in some future. Before any weighable

>stone is laid, unbending
>>support raised, centuries
>>trusted, these are complete.
"So you have spatial nightmares?" someone asks.
No, always they are

>ecstatic. One is *there*,
>>in the building, the structuring air
>>pressing back, upshooting
buttresses or nautiloid partitions.
And the way I stand in the visions?

>Among many dissimilar storeys
>>and stairways, unbuilt
>>but near to the foot—
which lifts me, with no scuff and less speed,
level to level.

Bedrooms

Who are you, coming without flash and standing high
on a chair in the doorway?
—And who are you, living in this room
these twenty years,
testy and messy,
pitching bibelots
more from weariness than from anger—
but casting things aside for
charity, too?
Flannel shadows, caning, a clear
old mirror whose "flaws"
avert the eye
around to the present
shiftiness of surviving—
I see them where you live, do you?

Once I saw a horse
rearing so as to fit
in a tall glass cabinet
in a small bedroom south
of Aliceville, Alabama—
Gladys Hudson's ceramic palomino
among salvaged,
crocheted, framed
fandangles, shaken rugs,
hand-twisted chintz
chrysanthemums.
A horse. And I have
no picture . . .

In a book, in the dark, at the thinking end of one bedframe,
this passage, memorized:
A loon swims
leisurely in the heart of the stream—

seeming to certify
the solitude of the place.
Who is that flat person
slow-kicking with the loon
to rest—
while the green reserve of the unforgotten
is thicker and stiffer
than pages of memoir, more rigorous
than any camera wall?
Is it something to share,
the dream one hopes
will be so comfortingly spectacular?

The light a photographer pinpoints
is for diary writing,
drawer handles, hide-soled slippers,
a single pair.
It says, *I can't*
go on being where you are.
But look close
at the dark
in this actual square
of your life.
I give you back your dream room.
You hallucinate beyond me here.

2

Trails

Waiting for Lesser Duckweed:
On a Proposal of Issa's

December, a weekday,
no one else crossing
    (by way of the wet path)

the bird sanctuary's yellow
spongy bottomland,
    no duckweed

any longer willow-green—
for now, the almost smoldering
    gas-lacy water says,

it's down making turions.
The way to be introduced to it
    is first

to meet nothing. In rain,
a thin microscope-specimen rain.
    One raises a face

to flooded sketchlike
territories of trees,
    sepia, seeping;

to blunt, upward bluffs of ivy,
bared poison oak;
    a soaking place,

fed by springs and floods,
shallow water table
    strained by willows.

In spring, in a more forward month,
yellow-red willow-bud husks
   will sharpen the trail,

their old pen tips,
oleo-spot gulls' beaks,
    brighten the flat brown pond,

and a man with a knife,
whack, whack,
    righthanded down the path,

will kill new twigs too new
yet to be woody.
    But there's

no duckweed until the summer
when finally where a creek
    swims in,

    there's duckweed
barely tugging
the moss-strandy bottom,

    wheatcolored
seed-shrimps
touring in and around

    the barbless roots,
hyaline drag-lines,
where a mud-smooth leech adjusts

    and tows
the duckweed a bit.
Some places it bunches,

simple but chained,
a soft hauberk on the stream.
Some places it wrinkles,

a basilisk's back.
It is utterly simple
and multiple.

It is floating,
one of many rafts.
The water here is cold,

fresh, still
and hard. Ovals, ovals.
"Let's take the duckweed way

to clouds,"
said Issa. Let's take it
when it comes to us,

its leaf
not called a leaf,
diameter for which there is no term

but green;
let's follow
the least weed up

to nimbuses
however many
steps it takes,

late in the day's
rootless endurance
to make much progress

the duckweed way.
Let us grow and wane
with this ideal, the way

it keeps the single petal
of its bloom confidential
in a hollow on its side.

Lemna minor

with thanks to Lucien Stryk,
who translated

In Memory of the Surprised

Richter Scale 7.1, October 17, 1989

A shin-high zoo goat stood on a sheep;
a fish seemed to look up and question us.
That was on solid ground,
in even water.

Since then, they have experienced
the breaking wave, the bucking wool,
those seconds when my mother's clock
was breaking, breaking southward,

her chimer with the painted spider,
plunging—no silk to slow it—
from its ledge.
And the rising birds

of my birthmother's letters
("male Nuttall's Woodpecker bathing!")
flew in safety over apricots and oaks
as deaths

were counted—
people alone and people together.
Hostile, benighting, sun-fallen dreams
erected and destroyed

their balconies and mezzanines
that night until we woke, stelae, shocked
stone, petrified but rolled together.
You shuddered once, a separate time,

as we were out walking. You said it was autumn
entering all of you.

I saw it: your strata mystifying
all the way down. It caused no damage

or did it? At that moment
you were shining (though like a hummingbird—
never in right light for viewers to tell
which color's where),

feeling the incision
of earth turning its past under,
its zeal's occasion only a season,
no houses kneeling yet you foreseeing

a world without you or us or anyone.
The shiver was stunning,
as if the drying coastal pearly everlasting
ghosted through you, with warbler-yellow

broom the lame deer at evening
gnawed bluntly as a novice gardener. . . .
Is it universal solitude
on a spine? and how can that be?

But we know where else it lodges, have seen it
moor in gilt seams
up a teenage egret's legs,
catch under the wings of a landing harrier

about to taste the falling temperature
—of some being—; and on a given dive
through necklaces or toolsheds of chains
of kelp, the harbor seal's face

shows, in arcs of perplexed reflections,
the rush of adjustment.
All the haunted now—enormous company
as what you feel flies back to its source

having found you chilled, filled
you with sympathy, connected
the indwelled look in your eyes to the many
shattered windows facing the sea.

Coastscape and Mr. Begley

One eighth of an inch across—
one petal of the yellow field.

Or each with a green strap narrower
than a hospital bracelet, sedges

raise the height of a marsh.
The entire estuary could leak

drop by drop through cupped hands,
egret's beak, or a shed's mossy roof as rain.

Beyond, grain by grain,
subjewelry, the sand—

rock in note form.
On the cliff top, thrift: "dense terminal head

on naked stalk." Or "naked
foot stalking" the sea's chamber?

And poppies: "But colorless. Colorless"—?
No, carotid, perilous, couldn't be less

like business.
Jag by jag

the poison hemlock's leaves. Then bulrushes'
readjustments

as nested redwings scare.
A blackbird is flying into a heron's tail—

plucking and punching, it bides
there for a second

of a second, pulling a quill or,
deeper, the hind-flesh,

and the heron does not fly
or swing around, but bears

its eye lonelier,
steps in a glide

from shallows to shore
to where the helm goose of a flock

lowers its neck
in a curl of rejection.

And the million barbules
of the Great Blue vanish

into a summer fog of panicles,
gold-green, gray-lavender spikelets

of tufted hairgrass, spreading lovegrass.
Woman, this is the landscape all through which

you have left your sight,
your sight you dropped as a car

came rushing toward you, your flawed mediums
to which you paired binoculars;

your wet living lenses trained
above each nasturtium (close your eyes,

you get a morning glory),
your sight with which you measured creek depth

through dark glasses, your vision you
broke to shoals of smashed cast-ups at the strandline.

All through these floatings you have left
your invisible seeing

that counted seventy-four fishing boats,
thirty-five brown pelicans,

seventy kites on one string,
sixty-five pocketed keepsakes from the sea.

Your scanning
is transported with the sand

from beach to beach, deposited in an ocean canyon
no one has ever seen, where in privacy you can hear

the panoramic sounds break down:
the lisping bubbles

fly apart, pods chatter
in the yellow lupine, the snake your foot tips off

escape, the heron's silence—
conscientious, exposed.

Then you hear Mr. Begley's voice,
each little botanical correction.

"I am a painter," he says.
Certainly he has known the landscape

by the eighth-inch. Skunkweed's pomander
is caught on his fly-line. Socrates

is dying in his umbelliferae. And
everything immediate to him is small: Bees carry

landscape on them, birds drop it
from the air; filaree

miniaturizes war; damselfly hovers
gratified as a needle over a new seam

or a tearing about to mend.
Little pimpernel hotspots,

hatched and housecleaned cliff swallows' eggs
bloodsplattered as a man's bad shave,

dunegrasses' half-circle sweeps
sanding away woodgrain of homes.

Antique ink on butterflies.
"Because I paint," Mr. Begley said. Good for him—

I have no excuse for looking.

Research Trail, Cold Canyon, November

Solano County

Direction: bronze knee-snagging flower-head,
unsprung from the weathered bank.

Direction down: bird; bird song
^^_____> . .

Direction utterly still:
longstanding gold lichens on boulders.

Or late, late: flicker, sunset feather-ribs.
Or passage under: soft holes in the trail—everywhere, burrows.

Re-routing: arrowhead wedge of muskrat or possum skull,
a jewel-box with teeth for clasp.

Aim as it says? Course up: hillrise—its associates,
manzanita, blue oak, digger pine, buckeye.

The pitch of a slope
suddenly too breakneck,

root, shoe, sole-slip, but just above that,
cinch, thinkable again.

Back to the carcass: desiccated muscle of a tail—
broken leather watchband.

It looks like an abrupt little dinosaur,
hair bedding thrown off to wake it.

Throw cover back over. Slip back to the pitch
of the hill: plant tibias, skeletal fall

village of spring's old plants,
a snit of framed junked sketches of lupine, finished fennel, seeded
    mustard.

Sociogeology: an artist's landfill.
Climbing upslope more slowly than fire, scraping through

dried yarrow foam, I hear the quick side-changing
of opposite hummingbirds.

Fire gate. Listen for: California thrasher, northern pygmy owl,
white-throated swift, warblers, flycatchers. Listen for fire.

Bones and leather: Could it have been
"the rare cinnamon opossum"?

Skunks nibble on dead ones.
Muskrat has webbed feet

but similar tail—it's
"reddish to dark brown," shorter than possum.

Possums climb a tree "to eat a ripe persimmon."
Confusing book sketches dusky-footed wood rat.

Those white claws and silk boots = muskrat. Hind feet
partially webbed. Swims backward

or forward with ease.
Fox, cougar, or owl may have got it.

"Their interesting mouths
remain shut to water

while the incisors, out front,
munch away at succulent underwater stems." Did I see

an underwater mouth?
But it pointed *here*: I'm stone-benched in an abounding dried garden

of giant paper leaves
neither shrunken nor crushed (the deer keeping to their path).

I'm sitting in the tall
dried ray-flowers, pine-board-faded-whiskey color,

their involucres flying, dried waving their gold.
In circles of basal leaves

the size of many eagle-feather headdresses
laid on the ground, hill-skirts.

I sit among preserved whisks
of itinerant air, the ears of the rise.

Wyethia angustifolia: mule's ears: "Calf Compass-Plant":
"An innate love for the mysterious and poetical

makes people wish to believe
in strange and beautiful tales"

that claim its leaves stand edges always
pointing N & S. "When beauty achieves great subtlety,

the Japanese call the effect *shibui*—
restrained elegance

only time can reveal, an aged tea, scenery
of a gray, brown, or moss-green color, the impression

one gets from looking at the face
of a certain kind of older person."

"The end of growth, the final stage"
parched, above the rushing island-making stream.

Someone said: "You're between books."
As if you could ever be at one,

as you are never "at" a trail.
I look at my unsure feet: All millennial support is for the garden,

for the wildest. Then look away: Did you see
the creekside cormorant spiral?—three times—widely—

just to clear the 300′ dam.
As if, when you arrive here, you become one of the old folk,

your colors having been green passing, ripe black
purpling, pale and crimped, yellowed, goldened, drabbed,

aired. You are very, very old,
and people shaped like arrowheads

find such preservation as you are
in the dry garden. The stone tools find you, their museum.

Look, I say to myself turning, the young
blue oaks are more earth's progeny now than I. They think

the winding needs the watch,
not otherwise.

Far away, in the ruins of civilizations,
earth colors crawl from frescoes.

The planet spins them off. The trail whirls into a helix of dust.
When I was in labor,

friends read me bleak poetry.
Read more, I harped, until a new thing turns our heads.

Path Through a Few Things that Must Be Said for Putah Creek, at the Foot of Monticello Dam

Before we know we are spun,
between the dam's spilled staircase
and dismaying face (a Venetian
blind holding back
an ocean)

and a violence
waiting for our trust
to turn its way,
we track down the old yellow canyon
of pipevine swallowtails,

pitch essence and effusions of anise,
and watch pines escalade out
from the flowing pathway:
The creek is governed. Violaceous *Brodiaea*
kicked high here, last month. Now, fennel

feathers low open places, bluegreen
etherous plumes surrounding
last year's silvery, or stannic, ghosts
of cellulose
like baskets of antique pens

saved for the half sentence of ink
left in each.
Buckeye's maybe-toxic clusters foam,
votive stadiums moot to bees.
Saw-toothed toyon blooms, bees

and variations all over it.
It fills in the gaunt rut

of the canyon.
Honeybees, toe-fat, tapshoe-shape,
test the waters and taste. They need

to recover the wet composition
of their bodies—
and species-memory: Like the dry
overland flight of a bee
across Saint

Helens' devastation,
miles between shrubs,
hours between dew,
how low it flew over ashes
without landings.

These bees go to the slaking ground
in its lapped, liquid, fast honey state.
As they lift away
from human impressions in the sand,
late morning light in the shallows

outlines a water strider's shadow—
the way a longhaired cat
nimbuses, searching a dirt road at dusk,
or a buck's backlit antler velvet
glows as he lowers, foraging

on a lupine hummock in the foredune.
Two skippers contact
and separate—six coal ovals
(as after theatrical lack of sleep, under eyes),
twelve, then six and six—

to the faint chaos of a sequence
of brief bell-like water-sounds,

like one-line piano compositions
by Donald Justice
(or one-line poems

in an inch-high issue
of *Dragonfly*, 1972).
The water is the churned green
of my birthfather's last cup
of morphine

as I saw it two
days later through his door.
And the current is cold
below its sunburnt top-water.
If over this slow-sided, fast-centered creek flying

insects graph a transparent map,
faster still a swallow's life
consists in devouring the backroads,
the dashed ones,
off that map

one route at a time.
Orbit consuming byway.
Flight-paths almost become visible:
pointed-winged parabolas
like a hook

full of thin years of belts
falling to the closet floor.
The swallows move on; the tangle
stays in the eyes.
And as we come out of the canyon,

flow
away and on,

somehow in this time,
in minutes we lost,
someone has abandoned

a stolen Mazda
and ripped parts from it,
not closed the doors
or trunk,
has undone the tires,

left the car
unadorned,
Quaker,
its idling trembles
gone. They pass into me.

I am antique with fear,
recoiling from but mulling
branched lines of the fractured windshield,
headlights and reflectors,
their light beaten

out of them, crumpled.
The scene is not stranger than the way
one visionary schizophrenic ruins
a holy city painting
with jealous ravings

or beloved Jeffers jolts
every sublime
seascape with rage.
I don't know what will take
the car's carcass over,

my terrified incomprehension
over;

I don't know how we end up feeling
better from worse
when the mechanism's gone—

but we leave,
cross the bridge
(and its county line sign)
above the suspended pueblo
of the cliff swallows,

the gates of their adobe
abodes made of creek-water,
grit, and mud of dust
from which fennel fledges herb-winged
and pine ascends, nourished.

Dominion—death has it, beauty has it,
water has it, drought
has it. Within the cells of peace
war is jailed or escapes,
violent with thieves.

And, their barium chloride
fireworks backs
dazzling us even in memory,
the violet-green
swallows fly up, up

to take over the woodpecker holes.

Paths Rounding Timberline, Mt. Hood, Last Week of Summer

All-mantling, the grit—
scoured and beaten
and rinsed
   by glacier sap,

ranging over scrubbed slope sides
batting off
the sun,
   the previous million

snows, the engraving
summer rains,
clean rock
   to eat—

not like dust,
not like zest
shaved and bowled on a table
   to taste,

but an ascendant
snack
of rock essence,
   its core

of dryness
crisp-cased,
a spark on the teeth.
   Shock of stone-flash,

an ember to float
on meltwater's first

gradual toe
   descending

through its old evaporated channel,
stone-bundled bed
flowering
   with asters,

half-pint yarrow,
buckwheat,
that only yesterday
   yesterday's rationed thaw-water flowed through

and evanesced from
later in the dark
when the summit's snow-
   pack shivered,

stiffened,
tightened its spring.
A high place
   with a crunch,

arching underfoot,
hollowing the lungs.
Bell music
   of pumice

as a foot
scuffs the trail.
("A rock talks
   to a rock,"

the preacher
woman sings.)
A rock rings,
   not ash but orchestra.

We've left
heron-blue whitebark pine trunks
long dead but reaching,
   dwarf lupines,

very approachable trees.
We've left
smooth purple
   cones in clusters

of ten, thick as valley grapes
outweighing
the cruciform vine.
   Purpler

than the grit.
Sound of a fly.
Small moth
   on the flowers. Slightly

larger orange peel
butterfly. Click rhythm
of grasshopper.
   Spider

silks blowing
from stunted spruce.
Ground-sprawled fir,
   a starry

starry
mountain
hemlock.
   And exactly

as we cross
a tiny runoff

stream bed—
   2:40 p.m.—

first waters of the flow
meet us
and cross
   the path.

This first
water is slow.
Almost gelatinous.
   —So

tense. For later torrent
amasses
and sings clearly.
   We anoint

porcelain alpine foreheads
with an ashy drop.
The trickle takes a good
   fifteen minutes

to wet its path
across our path.
It turns
   some rocks gingery,

some
smoke-damaged green.
It picks up seeds
   and floats them.

They twirl around.
How almost like
a moon jelly
   on a beach

the water
quivering there
in timberline sand,
    the advance toe

of the stream being born.
Sip that water
in a one-ounce cup.
    Shouldn't.

But.
Clear, sweet,
the first drinker
    says. And look

where it will go,
to the bigger stream,
splashes firing up
    like sparks out of a log,

slapping boulders
while two
young women
    of the range's

first people
nap in the canyon,
on a blanket,
    in a deep

silver coulee
through under-andesite
and ashfall tuff.
    For this

short time, the old
snow's young again.

Later we clean
   pitch off our palms

with the ash grit.
An insect sings,
long trill,
   somewhere inside

an aster cluster.

Phlox Diffusa

A Poem for My Fiftieth Birthday

Is it calm after midnight on its rocky slope,
exactly fitted to its nice little rubble?
Easy to think it's a bedtime slipper of a flower, owning no boots.
It lies flat on its back and looks at stars.

"Undaunted by stern surroundings," Mary Elizabeth Parsons says
in *The Wild Flowers of California*, 1907.
Like the game pummeled seapalm on outer rocks in breakers
the phlox spreads happy in its xeric meadow.

The flowers completely hide the leaf cushion,
the way a lot of enthusiams obscure
the inner idiot. Actually clothe it,
but wildly as a shopping spree.

Charmed and usually older hikers want to lie right down beside it.
Starlike, delicate.

"The tiny crammed leaves live in a pocket of calm partly
of their own making, and there they trap
windblown particles
that slowly become a nourishing soil."

Taproots eight to fifteen feet.
A throw pillow bolted to granite.
Easy to think it's only three inches tall,
until you think of that, think of that root.

Bluegum: On the Curving Paths of Golden Gate Park

A deep blue layer of scent on the ground,
long scrolls of bark, fallings,
sickles and minisci of leaves on the path edges.

Lakewater loops: Each boat is trailed by a duck or two.
Nasturtiums climb the frame of a cascade.
Painters from a guild even out handmade papers,

light-running night scenes,
wet octopus, giant iris, tree in half a flail.
Tiers and catenas of roofs glitter sequenced across the hills.

Egret among remote-control yachts,
sailboats, steam vessels
to scale, arm-length submarines submersing.

Anthologies: As time goes on,
"new poets" move further toward
the front of the book, the "old" end.

I read of journeys to temples, shrines:
"Climbing to the Monastery of Perception,"
"Visiting the Chan Master Chengru & the Kalapati Xiao

at Their Hermitage on Song Hillock,"
"Traveling to the Dwelling of Li, Man of the Mountains,
and Writing This on His Walls."

The water keeps gliding, crooking, elliptical.
On a stone stage: A pond slider, lifting its neck,
acts a still role among currents of boots and toes.

And all around the greenness and living fibrousness,
winds in the woods, feathers of fog and real feathers
in tops of cypresses, pines.

Mist-drip into ground. Perimeter
of houses the tints of beachcombings, shells turned
up or over, accordant white and peach-light calciums,

pale green nacres, hills of dwelling-shells
patterned after, paralleling, waves,
water-crests, and sea-fetch valleys. Rooms

tight, nearby and deposited, washed across distances, sanddollars
blanching, eateries with neon fish-markings
for the deep of night.

Wang Wei, translated, says,

> "When birds arrive
> he speaks of the Dharma again"

and

> "Before, this far away place
> just clung to rock amid cloud-mists:
> Today
> it is all around my pillow
> and mat. How
> can I stay just for a while?
> I should render service
> for an entire life."

And to whom? to what?
Here I am—old—
but I remember my life

from the time I learned of indelible ink,
just south, over that blue range white in fog.
But the surfaces it was written on—

silk labels, slick box lids,
lists for rain and mildew and illuminations that fade—
are speckles now and crumbs and wisps.

Service for life:

as red-beaded banks of toyon bolster the birds
and leather bergenia's moist leaves
soothe the rough newts.

Trail to the Farthest Spring, Mt. Hood, September

Farther than the last cistern,
where yet another final
      world's end pool
      collects, reflection

of a sky or self is bounded
on the upslope by fattest moss,
      golfhat chartreuse.
      It feels like a sweet,

misleadingly thug-bodied cat
when you pat it.
      Pressing back, it rubs
      with licked-fur undersides:

a wild mountain sponge.
And with pumice so at hand,
      this big tub cleanses
      a wilderness.

Beside it, a flying lesson
of penstemon, mauvette.
      Round rushes stuck all around,
      with serious man's-shoe-brown

pompons on their very tips.
I do not want to weigh beyond this pool.
      The land is high, sheer, bald,
      with all dislodgeable rocks.

In the cat's-cornea floor of the cistern,
the shadow of a man I know
      disrobes like Henry Vaughan
      dunked in this

"sacred wash and cleanser."
But as his flesh chills pure,
        a voice from the chasm
        we crossed to get here

starts roaring, muddying,
tripling its flow.
        It is 2:22 p.m., I check,
        as if 9 1 1. This new

flood's the rinse-water color
of an artist's brush
        made of sunburnt bear fur.
        Was lucid and lazy as an OED

magnifying glass before,
when we leapt it. The man
        I know better now
        dresses and leaps it.

It shouts beside him—an alp-melting release.
The channel begins to canyon,
        its throat gruff.
        The cathedral clock of ice

on the peak's south slope
makes melt its chime.
        For a moment I think
        if I ever come back here

this would be a place to sing.
An echo-odd, off-the-trail,
        deep volcanic sleep music
        liquefied and lullabyed from plain talk.

Whenever others sing,
in rooms between walls,

their cries still bear on places
far away. And it will be

not a woman's call
but lightning's or a rock's, a cloud's or crystal's,
        mountainous molecules
        choiring, hoarse.

And the song will find words,
something about around-boot grandeur,
        about how everyone bare
        is a timberline

that can go home,
down, down,
        a timberline in one's own home tub,
        knowing the song

of our heights this way.

Ocean Water Absorbs Red, Orange, and Yellow Light

in a flash
and allows only the green and blue
to penetrate the depths.
As we love deeply those we love,
they are our blue and green.

And what if
the sex so easily replaced by next
and next times is the last,
lapsing into the Dalai Lama's
"method of coping with lust":

Sometimes in
my dreams there are women. When such
dreams happen, immediately
I remember, "I am monk."
A tidal zone is like sex—

wet rocks
a flesh, the flexing of anemones
hung like cat balls, shoulder carryalls,
or hummingbird nests from outcrops,
seaweed bodies long together,

hanks, skeins,
warps, lariats, the paraphernalia of dead
ocean cheerleaders. The appearance
of a beautiful face, a body,
however beautiful, decomposes

to a skeleton.
The fffsss of wave-water lowers
into round gravel,

floods silver areolas of turban snails,
and dry flashes into wet—

When we penetrate
to human flesh and bones, NO
beauty, is there?
A couple in a sexual experience is happy
for that moment. Then very soon

trouble begins.
The holy man's viewpoint is before
one's born body chemicals
gladden the flesh and find for it
long moments within the seconds,

gasps
that replace clock-ticks. And he
should dream of profounder women,
or men, to make irrelevant
the slowing or quickening

of the skeleton,
however it drags in eternity.
"Deposit/withdrawal/deposit/withdrawal,"
the lover says of waves. You have
to love each other's

elements,
healthful calcium, the stone earbones
as delicate to seduction
as to fine mineral rain embedding
a fossil. And, like the field guide

for driftwood,
the feeling guide to human bones
can help identify why strong

light through countless self-
    absorbed literal

            (and even literary)
rosy-natured human nipples keeps on
        descending to these cores,
the bluegreen chassis inside
        the down-sworling body,

            the red
and yellow femurs surfaced together
        in the opened crypt
or tossed at last on shore
        among carnelians and agates drying,

            arousing
color when wet, even the inexpressive
        skull seen to be homely
as an ecstasy of gaping mouth
        returned to the wild

as the outermost open mind.

                    Marshall Gulch Beach, Sonoma coast

Genius of Fog at Ecola Creek Mouth

The horse meadow quarters roots as large
as if they'd cantered from the stable.
They lie in salt rush and spiky large-headed sedge.
They recline in bird's-foot trefoil
the horses crop. Loggers' drift-stumps,
they rave at the root end,
but on their misery-whipped plane
light springwood bands, dark summerwood rings,
weathered and fuzzed. Up to the woods of small alders,
they gallop in heavy recumbencies.
One swirling wooden mane holds a crow.

When fog in the spirit of blue harbor seal skin
suffuses this pasture, the great roots can't be told
from beings that change places;
and, superimposed, true horses, in fact, drift
from back in the nebula
to the immediate drizzly foreground,
with the dark burgeoning aspect of old growth logs
tumbled into seeds for birds.
The landscape is felted, hushed, as the line
of horses moves, sinew and tracheid, out to sea.

Crouched on the uprush edge, focusing low to the sand
and tracking coppery, tinny mica tracings—
jet, pewter, bronze, as if tannin gilded a fish-scale
or an oak leaf fell across a vein of pyrite—
I can only see up to the herd's approaching, jaunty knees.
Their burl-brown, spherule, liquid eyes
have not seen me. They are quieted by fog,
their riders as lofty as little trees.
When I evade, spring up like beach wood
twisted by a wave, I am not surprised

they go straight through my station
on the lacy swash.

Such dense luminosity—I inch back
to the inland of grayed black-blooded
Himalayan berries, silvered rummy pink spirea.
But fog makes it all one field of direction,
our bearings and our contours corresponding,
vaporous human torsos, humid pasterns,
fogged-in cannons and fetlocks, misty lungs,
and true fog-mind neither blurred nor mumbled,
amnesic nor censorious. Its genius is to be unafraid
so near breakers you cannot hear,
that do not roar in a climate so huge, diffuse,
and tender.

Edge Effect

Arcadia Beach, Oregon

Even under a petroglyphic coastal overcast,
the sand flushes with a heat almost innocent,
unhurt as it burns, and thus it is so often
the purest place for us as children.

Now, when we imprint its edge, we know it will wash.
While we may squint, its glint is broken lenses.
Rubbing sand in my palm, I feel
vision in that hand. I see

to reach outside the wet breathing ribcage
of the horizon. At my blind side,
basalt: shearable, towerable, and able to abide
long hours and average eons. The cliff

houses its resident eyes in caves,
in nests, down crevices, in hives. Ships,
if sensitive, may feel watched. And underfoot,
beneath goat-stepping wet opals of old toenails,

whole orbits of washed-in sea gooseberries
kindle a gaze up every few feet, glassies
convexing the vista, oculists' models of the eye's
hermaphroditic twin, paired in one single flesh

as we, with two eyes in one head, are mated for sight.
Merely to move forward, I tear draglines
of gull prints, their scuff's slight stickiness
to land before they fly. Beneath gulls' high ride,

every second villager's the best imagist
he or she can be for sea stacks' rough allure
offshore. It's all the brush-fingered seem to see.
Their garden or kitchen studios hatch water-slender

watercolors, stout sumi-e outlines, stolen styles—
expropriated eyes—of great but landlocked artists
of any continent but this. They line the palisades,
hold mirrors to the sea, even gladly to fog.

The whole subduction zone
calls painters for a briefing every day—
and every day the wet description dries.
But here, far up the littoral, I feel another congregation;

I sense they are inspecting everything going by.
Backbone, backbone, backbone
of stones: Stack three, you have a god: a minor one
improves on none. It's a beach outing

for a gang of almighties. Each has a base, a trunk, a head,
a jutting chin. Or driftwood eyebrows.
They are more than pillars, rock on rock.
One probes with seaweed field glasses, alert with poise

not of the spy but of the curious, of the
minerally secure: What's to be seen, its body
language says, in this shred of humanity coursing
north? I feel weather-cut edges of one watcher

multiply, its brain stones' ordained postures aiming
at the sea through any shore-searcher in the way.
I feel stone necks risen to attention, each vertebra
an observation deck. Against the cliff a pantheon.

No shadows on their cheeks, they are not grim.
Gray, they are not whimsy. They stand up stark.

What does "stark" mean anyway? Didn't Anne G. say
my father-in-law George's weightroom

"looked so stark"? Those dumbbells no longer made,
their deadweight laid out in increments
of hardship, increasing as hardship will, the barbells
propped like desolate businessmen at the final gate

of an airport concourse, present only to pick up
another drear and cunning company joe
whose name they hold penned on a pitiful placard. . . .
Stark. Can it mean pure? utter? simple? strong?

Sometimes I've seen eighty-year-old George standing
on his head, upside-down power, a restacking
of stones, right there on his gunboat-stern
cement basement floor, rebuilding, rearranging the cairn,

his body well-trained to be ancient, an Old World
stonemason. Why should bone be the most
solid-seeming part of a god around a mind?
Isn't a skull just a showcase for eyes? The fact that feet

in air come down, rocks tumble in time,
deduce to abdomen, thorax, small insect head,
almost back to diagram, that one
frost crystal brings the stone church to the ground,

excuses or defends erecting this toppler
while one can. Gods are hard. But longer life-tested sand
is soft. I hear one rock fall, the highest stone, on point,
fall backwards, and here we turn, we must turn, back,

as we would if we had any children with us,
not ready to take them beyond the falling of the gods
and yet permitting them to hear
the softness of their landings,

where wounds will bathe, bedded in sand,
one edge rushing over to enfold the other.

NOTES

The two compartments of this book, "Portrayals" and "Trails," seem to me to embrace almost secretly related worlds. An overlap suggests itself between the poetics of outdoor natural history and the artistic discoveries of self-taught, "Outsider," or folk painters and sculptors. I would hope that the trail poems, though not as continuous as, say, the Pacific Crest Trail, do link up often enough to form quite a significant trek.

"Painting Self-Portraits with the Wisdom Project Women": The Women's Wisdom Project of Sacramento, California, teaches women who are homeless, mentally ill, or recovering from addictions, to discover their strengths through art. Visitors are expected to paint along with them.

"Spirit Writings": J. B. Murry (1908–1988) was a mystical visionary artist, a native of Georgia.

"Reposoir": Mose Tolliver (b. 1915 or 1919) is an Alabama self-taught artist. A reposoir is a "tree or any other place where a loa [supernatural being in Voodoo; genie, demon, or spirit] is supposed to live" (Alfred Métraux, *Voodoo in Haiti*).

"Outsider: Minnie Evans": Evans (1892–1987) painted her dreams and waking visions while working as a gatekeeper at a public garden in North Carolina.

"Outsider: Juanita Rogers": Rogers (1934–1985) worked near Montgomery, Alabama. The quoted words are from her description of the background of one painting, "Egyptian World." She claimed an apparently imaginary patron, "Mr. Stonefish."

"Justin McCarthy, Naive": McCarthy was a self-taught artist, a single man, who received no recognition for his work until quite late in his life, when folk art supporters began to take him seriously.

"Lessons Learned from a Small Drawing by Victor Joseph Gatto, Self-Taught Artist": Gatto (1893–1965), an ex-boxer, lived and worked in New York City and Miami.

"Bluegum: On the Curving Paths of Golden Gate Park": Titles and quoted passages derive from Pauline Yu's *The Poetry of Wang Wei*, Indiana University Press, 1980.

"Ocean Water Absorbs Red, Orange, and Yellow Light": See E. Yale Dawson

and Michael S. Foster, *Seashore Plants of California*, University of California Press, ©
1982, pp 95–96:

> One of the most interesting features of these plants is their color. Al-
> though they contain green chlorophyll, that pigment is generally masked
> by other, so-called accessory, pigments, especially the red phycobilins. In
> brightly lighted intertidal habitats, the "mix" of pigments is so varied that
> dark purplish, olive, brownish, or blackish colors are observed and the
> beginner in phycology may assume some of the dark-pigmented or
> greenish forms to be brown or green algae. In well-shaded places or in
> deeper water, the red pigments predominate and the plants are almost
> invariably purple, pink, or red. This reflected red color results from the
> algal pigments absorbing green and blue light. This absorption aids
> growth in the dim and limited light of deep water, for water absorbs red,
> orange, and yellow light very quickly and allows only the green and blue
> to penetrate to depth. The red pigment is able to absorb this deeply pen-
> etrating light and permits some red seaweeds to live at depths greater than
> 90 m (300 ft). Since little or no red light is available at depths below 3 m
> (10 ft) and greens and blues are absorbed, red algae growing in the sub-
> tidal often appear black unless illuminated with artificial light.

"Genius of Fog at Ecola Creek Mouth": "Misery whip" is loggers' term for what
the dictionary calls a "lumberman's saw."

A C K N O W L E D G M E N T S

I am grateful to the following publishers, who first printed the poems in this collection:

The American Poetry Review: "Reposoir" and "In Memory of the Surprised"
The American Voice: "Painting Self-Portraits with the Wisdom Project Women"
Field: "Choosing an Author for Assurance in the Night" and "Spirit Writings"
Harvard Review (Spring 1995, no. 8): "Ocean Water Absorbs Red, Orange, and Yellow Light"
The Iowa Review: "Waiting for Lesser Duckweed: On a Proposal of Issa's"
The Kenyon Review (New Series, Winter 1994, vol. 16, no. 1): "Outsider: Minnie Evans" and "Outsider: Juanita Rogers"
The New Virginia Review: "Path Through a Few Things that Must Be Said for Putah Creek, at the Foot of Monticello Dam"
The New Yorker: "Eclipse Facsimile" and "Bedrooms"
The Paris Review: "Ode to Early Work"; "My Personal Hercules"; "Lessons Learned from a Small Drawing by Victor Joseph Gatto, Self-Taught Artist"
Poetry: "Affirmation Against Critics"; "The Study of Genius"; "The Clown"; "Genius of Fog at Ecola Creek Mouth"; "Research Trail, Cold Canyon, November"; "Edge Effect"
Poetry Ireland Review: "Justin McCarthy, Naive" and "Trail to the Farthest Spring, Mt. Hood, September"
The Southern Review: "Great Art, Great Criticism" and "Preliminary Designs"
TriQuarterly: "Bluegum: On the Curving Paths of Golden Gate Park"
The Yale Review: "Coastscape and Mr. Begley"; "Paths Rounding Timberline, Mt. Hood, Last Week of Summer"; "Phlox Diffusa"

"Choosing an Author for Assurance in the Night" and "Waiting for Lesser Duckweed: On a Proposal of Issa's" also appeared in *The Best American Poetry* 1992 and 1993, respectively.

For permission to reprint the epigraphs, I am grateful to Gene Epstein of the Epstein/Powell Gallery, New York City, and to University of California Press for passages from Allan A. Schoenherr's *A Natural History of California*, © 1992 by The Regents of the University of California. The dialogue from "The Oprah Winfrey Show" is reprinted with permission of Harpo Productions, Inc.

University Press of New England

publishes books under its own imprint and is the publisher for Brandeis University Press, Dartmouth College, Middlebury College Press, University of New Hampshire, University of Rhode Island, Tufts University, University of Vermont, Wesleyan University Press, and Salzburg Seminar.

About the Author

Sandra McPherson is the author of twelve books of poetry, most recently *The Spaces Between Birds* (Wesleyan, 1996) and *The God of Indeterminacy* (Illinois, 1993). Her book *The Year of Our Birth* (Ecco, 1978) was nominated for the National Book Award and she has been featured on the Bill Moyers series *The Language of Life*. She is Professor of English at the University of California, Davis.

Library of Congress Cataloging-in-Publication Data

McPherson, Sandra.
    Edge effect : trails and portrayals / Sandra McPherson.
       p.   cm. — (Wesleyan poetry)
    ISBN 0–8195–2225–2 (alk. paper). — ISBN 0–8195–2226–0 (pbk. : alk. paper)
      I. Title. II. Series: Wesleyan poetry program.
    PS3563.A326E34   1996
811'.54—DC20   95–33661